Let Us Pray

By James R. Mitchell

C.S.S. Publishing Company, Inc.
Lima, Ohio

LET US PRAY

Copyright © 1991 by
The C.S.S. Publishing Company, Inc.
Lima, Ohio

Library of Congress Cataloging-in-Publication Data
Mitchell, Jim, 1933-
    Let us pray: five sermons, object lessons, and orders of service
on prayer / by Jim Mitchell.
        p.   cm.
    ISBN 1-55673-291-0
    1. Prayer—Christianity—Sermons.   2. Congregational churches—
Sermons.   3. Sermons, American.   4. Worship programs.
5. Children's sermons.   I. Title.
BF213.M53   1991
248.3'2—dc20   90-48918
                                                                    CIP

9124 / ISBN 1-55673-291-0   PRINTED IN U.S.A.

These sermons on prayer are dedicated to the members of the Monday Evening Prayer Group, which met regularly from 1976 to 1980 at the First Congregational Church of Wilmette, Illinois (UCC). In their company and with their help I learned what it means to address and be addressed by the living God whose justice and mercy never fail and whose peace passes all understanding.

James R. Mitchell

Table of Contents

Prayer of Meditation (read silently)

Preserve me, O God, for in thee I take refuge. I bless the Lord who gives me counsel . . . I keep the Lord always before me; because he is at my right hand, I shall not be moved. Therefore my heart is glad, and my soul rejoices; my body also dwells secure . . . Thou dost show me the path of life; in thy presence there is fullness of joy, in thy right hand are pleasures for evermore. (Psalm 16:1, 7-9, 11)

Prelude

Call to Worship

Hymn ''O Day of Rest and Gladness''

Call to Confession

Unison Prayer of Confession

God of grace and God of glory, we acknowledge that we often focus our attention on the darker side of life. We allow ourselves to be weighed down and depressed by the evil of the world and by our own failures and shortcomings. We forget that in Jesus Christ you have overcome death, defeated the power of evil and redeemed us from the grasp of sin. Teach us to respond to your grace with joy and gratitude. Fill our hearts with faith, hope, courage and joy. Fill us with Holy Joy and gratitude. Amen.

Assurance of Pardon

***Gloria Patri**

Children's Sermon

***Hymn** "Lord Enthroned in Heavenly Splendor"

Prayer of the Pastor and People

The Lord's Prayer

Anthem

Scripture Readings
   1 Kings 3:5-9   Matthew 6:7-15   Romans 8:26-27

Sermon "Why Should We Pray?"

Silent Prayer

Offering
   Offertory
   *Doxology

***Hymn** "Immortal Love Forever"

Benediction

***Postlude**

*indicates the congregation is to stand

Why Should We Pray?

Nothing is more important in our spiritual life than prayer.

Worship is important, but without prayer worship becomes an empty and hollow occasion.

The sacraments of baptism and holy communion are of vital importance, but without prayer they become sterile rituals which have lost their vital connection to our lives.

Reading the Scripture is important, but without prayer the Bible is only an ancient and obscure text which puzzles and troubles but does not enlighten or guide us.

The indispensable element which connects worship, sacrament and scripture with the reality of human life is prayer. Prayer is the atmosphere within which our spiritual life lives and breathes. Without prayer faith suffocates and dies. Prayer is our address to God and God's address to us. Prayer, in the words of Dr. Perry LeFever, is that speaking which is also listening. It is a pleading which evokes acceptance. It is a passionate cry which brings deep inner peace. Prayer is that personal encounter with God which gives meaning, strength, comfort and joy to life. Telling people why they should pray is a little like telling people why they should eat or breathe or see. God is the source and destiny of our life; therefore we pray to live. We pray because we are invited and commanded to pray. We pray because God speaks in and through our prayer.

During the next few Sundays we are going to consider prayer from different aspects: the reasons why we pray; the obstacles to prayer; the consequences of prayer; and what we should pray for.

We do need to talk frankly about the need for prayer because, for many people in this post-modern, activity-oriented, achievement-oriented and possession-oriented world, prayer seems like a waste of time.

There are in fact as many reasons for prayer as there are persons praying. People bring to prayer their own needs, concerns, doubts, fears and hopes. But it is also true that there are four specific reasons which hold true in almost every life.

First, we pray to discover the will of God for our lives.

Second, we pray to gain perspective on our own life.

Third, we pray to achieve peace of mind.

Fourth, we pray to strengthen our spiritual connection with those around us.

Prayer enables us to discover the will of God for our own lives. A basic question we all have to face is what we are going to do with our talents, abilities, skills and gifts. The answer to that question will determine the course of our life. Energy, skill, talent and brains can be used for good purposes or bad. They can be used to make the world a better place or they can be used to serve our own selfish and narrow ends with little concern for God or neighbor. In the end, what we do with what we have is just as important — perhaps more important — than our skills, intelligence or general aptitude. Prayer is the way we address that question with all the intensity, passion, and sincerity we can muster to ourselves and to God. It is only as we try to explain to God what it is that we think we are supposed to be doing with our life, that we can hear our own desires, intentions and motives. In prayer God speaks to us by enabling us to really hear ourselves. God's word spoken to us in prayer makes us aware of the meaning and possibilities of our life. In prayer we understand that life is a gift and a trust. In prayer we feel the seriousness of our life and the responsibility for making good use of whatever it is we have been given — whether it be much or little.

Prayer not only sets us on the right track; it also keeps us there. Prayer is a way of checking our course and making sure that what we are doing is leading us along the path that God has chosen for us. In prayer God reminds us that our life must always be lived for the best that we know. Prayer does not give us the answer to every specific question we have about how we are to live, but it can certainly give direction to our life.

Second, prayer enables us to gain perspective on our life. Prayer involves the experience of the transcendent reality of God. In prayer we stand before the presence of that mysterious, powerful and loving Other who is the origin and destiny of our life. In that encounter we realize, in a way that is otherwise impossible, that our desires, our comfort and our ambitions are not the hinge on which the universe turns. The Psalmist exclaims: ". . . what is man that thou dost regard him and the son of man that thou dost think of him? Man is like a breath, his days are like a passing shadow." Psalm 144:33-34. Isaiah proclaims that "All flesh is grass, and all its beauty is like the flower of the field . . . . The grass withers, the flower fades but the Word of our God will stand forever." Eventually, we all come to discover the unimportance of our own desires and ambitions. Death finally forces us to acknowledge that a life which is self-centered, self-directed and which tries to be self-sufficient is finally self-defeating. Prayer enables us to discover that truth before we have misdirected and wasted our life and while there is still time to make our life count. In prayer we also discover that even the tiny and transient specks of life which burn so briefly within each of us can be valuable and important if they are lived with God and for God.

Third, prayer gives us peace of mind. When we understand the will of God for our lives and that the value and importance of our life depend on our relationship to God, we also realize we are really safe. We know that our life can and does have importance and value because it is cherished and valued by God. Prayer helps us know that because of the power of God's love, we are and always will be utterly, completely and entirely safe. In prayer we know our safety does not depend on what we are doing for God but on what God has done and will continue to do for us. In prayer we can know that

Paul's words in Romans are addressed to us: nothing can separate us from the love of God in Christ Jesus. Because it is that love which is the supreme value and jewel of our life, we know that we are, in Reinhold Niebuhr's phrase, "beyond tragedy." Prayer leaves us with a feeling of quiet, peace and tranquility. We become centered. Prayer is like a soothing and refreshing hand which God lays upon the anxiety and frantic activity of our life.

Finally, prayer is the way we strengthen our spiritual connection with those around us. We pray for others and they pray for us. To pray for someone is to hold them in genuine concern. Prayer brings us closer to others. Prayer results in deeds of compassion and helpfulness. Prayer makes us compassionate persons and turns that compassion into concrete acts of helpfulness. In that mutual concern, compassion and solidarity, we are strengthened and supported. Pain shared is pain reduced and made bearable.

Prayer is the means by which God restores us to our true self, to the self which was created in the image of God and which is reconciled to its human limitations and to God. Prayer is the balm which heals the wounds and brokenness of human life and makes us truly alive and whole. Prayer is the life raft which carries us to salvation. Prayer enables us to speak to God and enables us to hear God speaking to us. Prayer gives us a purpose which cannot be shaken; a perspective which is both honest and joyful; a peace of mind which sustains us in the midst of all pain and sorrow; and a compassion which sees the face of Christ in the need of our neighbor.

Why should we pray? We pray because we can and we must if we are to be the truly human persons that God calls us to be. Let us pray:

God of love, majesty and power: Teach us to pray. Enable us to speak to you. Enable us to hear your voice and know your will. Make us the men and women that you would have us be. Amen.

Why Should We Pray?

Texts to think about: Psalm 42; Isaiah 6:1-8; 1 Samuel 3:1-10; Philippians 4:4-7; 2 Corinthians 1:11

1. Are there times in your life when you feel a deep need for God — when you ''long'' for God?

2. How has prayer helped you decide what to do with your life? How did you pray and how was your prayer answered?

3. How has prayer influenced you in the choice of your life's work? If you have not prayed for direction in finding a vocation, do you think that your life might have been different if you had?

4. Do you ask for guidance and direction in how to spend your leisure time? How has prayer influenced the way you spend your leisure time? If you were to make leisure a subject of prayer, how might that affect the amount of leisure that you have and what you do with that leisure? Can prayer help the ''workaholic'' to recover?

5. Has prayer influenced you in the way you do your life's work? Has prayer influenced your relationships with others at work? Has prayer influenced your standards of performance at work? Has prayer influenced what you think about your work life and your life at work?

6. Has prayer helped you in meeting specific problems in your work?

7. Do you pray about the everyday tasks and activities of life — cleaning the house, cooking, child care, maintenance, doing repairs, yard work — that are a part of every life? Has prayer helped you go about these daily tasks? Has prayer changed your attitude about the ordinary tasks of daily life?

8. The sermon speaks of a sense of "quiet, peace and tranquility" resulting from prayer. How and when has that been your experience? Are there times when you have not felt peace of mind as a result of prayer but instead felt energized, motivated, driven to action?

9. How has prayer made you aware of God's love? Has that awareness come through prayer itself or through the answers to your prayers?

10. How do you experience the love of God in your life and how is that experience enhanced by prayer?

11. How have your prayers for others changed your relationship to those persons? Do you tell the persons for whom you are praying that you are doing so? Does this make a difference?

12. Are there times when others have prayed for you? How did those prayers change your relationship with the person praying on your behalf?

13. How has God used prayer in your life to change your relationships with others? Has prayer helped you end destructive relationships in your life? Has prayer helped you form constructive and responsible relationships? Has prayer helped you to be reconciled to those with whom you were angry?

14. How does prayer enhance your compassion and your awareness of the problems and difficulties of others?

Why Should We Pray?

George was a 10-year-old boy who lived with his mom and dad and a dog named "Dash." George was having a hard time making up his mind about whether he should try out for the summer school band or whether he would rather play baseball. It was hard to decide. He thought he would like to play in the band. Music seemed like fun. He could see himself with a gleaming trumpet marching down the street in front of cheering crowds during the Fourth of July parade. Baseball seemed like fun, too. George could see himself standing at home plate, with the bases loaded and the opposing pitcher winding up. He could see the ball in his mind's eye — as big as a balloon hanging over home plate. He could hear the crack of the bat and feel the sting in his hands as the ball disappeared over the fence. It was tough to decide. Tomorrow was the last day to sign up for summer band.

So that night he sat down and had a long talk with mom and dad. "What should I do?" he asked. "How much are you willing to work to be a good musician?" dad asked. "And what if you don't hit any home runs? What if you end up playing in right field?" George hadn't thought about that. That night when George went to bed and said his prayers he asked God to help him make up his mind and to do what was best for him and his friends.

When George woke up the next morning he knew what he wanted to do. George didn't sign up for summer band that year. It would have been fun but he finally decided that he really wanted to play ball more than learn to play the horn. His talk with mom and dad helped him make up his mind.

We have a Heavenly Father to whom we can talk when we need to make up our mind about what we are going to do. God helps us decide what is right for us and what is best for all those around us. When you need to decide what to do I hope you will talk to God in prayer and talk to your moms and dads as well.

Prayer of Meditation (read silently)

The heavens are telling the glory of God; and the firmament proclaims his handiwork. Day to day pours forth speech, and night to night declares knowledge. There is no speech, nor are there words; their voice is not heard; yet their voice goes out through all the earth, and their words to the end of the world . . . But who can discern his errors? Clear thou me from hidden faults. Keep back thy servant also from presumptuous sins; let them not have dominion over me! . . . Let the words of my mouth and the meditation of my heart be acceptable in thy sight, O Lord, my rock and my redeemer (Psalm 19:1-14).

Prelude

Introit

Call to Worship

Hymn "This Day In Thy Dear Name We Meet"

Call to Confession

Unison Prayer of Confession

Gracious and loving God, you have invited us to speak to you and to hear your Word. Yet we fear the very encounter which could save and redeem us. We say our prayers are not answered. In truth, we refuse to pray because we are afraid you will answer our prayer and we will no longer be able to live for ourselves. Give us the courage, the trust and the commitment to open our ears and let you speak to us. Amen.

Assurance of Pardon

***Gloria Patri**

Children's Sermon

***Hymn** "Sweet Hour of Prayer"

Announcements

Prayer of the Pastor and People

The Lord's Prayer

Anthem

Scripture Readings
Luke 20:45-47   1 Chronicles 29:10-19   Romans 12:12

Sermon "Obstacles To Prayer"

Silent Prayer

Offering
Offertory
*Doxology

Hymn "A Mighty Fortress is Our God"

Benediction

Choral Response (congregation seated)

*Postlude

*indicates the congregation is to stand

Obstacles To Prayer

If the reasons for prayer are so compelling, why do we have so much difficulty in bringing ourselves to prayer? Why this reserve, this hesitation, this avoidance that we all sometimes experience?

The basic reason is simple but unpleasant: we are all sinners. We do not want to serve God but the demands of our own ego. We hide from our sin and from God. Sin and self-deception go together like bread and butter. The Gospel of John says: "For everyone who does evil hates the light, and does not come to the light, lest his deeds should be exposed." John 3:20. Real prayer always involves self-disclosure and self-recognition. Put another way, all real prayer involves confession. Confession is always painful and disturbing. Apart from the assurance of pardon which we have in the grace of Jesus Christ it is intolerably painful and disturbing.

There is a story about a beautiful young girl who married a dashing young soldier at the beginning of the Civil War. After a few brief weeks together, he marched off down the road and she remained standing in the lane waving goodbye. That road led to places like Fredericksburg, Manassas, Gettysburg and the Wilderness — and eventually to a soldier's death. When the telegram arrived from the War Department notifying the young bride of her husband's death in combat, she sensed what it was. But she refused to open it because she believed that by doing so she could avoid the painful reality of death and keep her husband alive. So she placed the unopened telegram on the dresser and never touched it again. After many years she, too, died, an embittered and psychotic old woman, a victim of her own self-deception and avoidance which poisoned her life more deeply and tragically than grief for a lost husband could ever have done.

In part, we avoid prayer for the same reason the young bride refused to open the telegram. We fear the pain we will experience if the truth about our own life is disclosed to ourselves and to God. We rationalize our failure to pray. The tragedy is that it is the avoidance of reality, of prayer, of judgment and grace — the avoidance of God, the flight from God — which proves to be really destructive in our lives. We flee the very encounter with God which could heal and save us.

This morning I want to address some of the rationalizations we use to avoid prayer. If we can expose these rationalizations for what they are, perhaps we can confront more honestly the dread we have of prayer and of the salvation which is its promise and its goal.

There are four common rationalizations used to avoid prayer. First, it is said that prayer is a form of magic which is beneath the intelligence of modern men and women. Second, it is said that prayer is useless because it is unanswered. Third, it is said that God already knows what we and others need so that prayer is unnecessary. Finally it is said that our time would be better spent working and thinking than in prayer; that prayer is a form of infantile escape from the tasks of the world and of life. Let us take a moment to examine these rationalizations before we turn to the deeper problem.

First, prayer is not magic. Magic is the use of ritual actions to control the natural world in accordance with our desires. Magic is really a form of primitive science because it is a way of manipulating nature. Prayer is speaking and listening to God and has as its primary focus our relationship with God. Prayer may involve petitions which concern the external world but it is primarily concerned with our relationship with God. Real prayer involves an encounter with God which always and necessarily changes human life. Magic is sometimes entertaining but it is always illusory. Prayer confronts us with truth and reality. Magic and prayer are radically different in their goals, methods and results.

Second, real prayer, sincere prayer, passionate prayer, is always answered. God always hears our prayer and God always answers our prayer, provided only that it is genuine. What the objection really means is that God does not always give us what we want. At bottom the objective is based on a childish and ego-centered understanding of God as a cosmic genie whose task is to serve our desires and wishes. I believe that God sometimes does grant even our childish wishes — not for the sake of our desires but because God can see that the granting of a particular petition is the way to move us toward the salvation of our soul. But whether particular petitions are or are not granted, God always responds. God answers prayer by giving us a conviction as to what we are to do with our lives. God answers our prayer by taking away the burden of anxiety and disquiet. God answers our prayer by forgiving our weakness and our shortcomings and by restoring our relationship with the divine ground of our being. God answers our prayer by placing in our hearts the compassion which finds expression in deeds of practical assistance. God always answers prayer.

Third, God does indeed know what we need and what others need. We do not pray to inform God of concerns which would otherwise be unknown to the Lord. We pray — we petition and ask — because we need to hear ourselves explain our requests to God. We pray because no human thought is complete until it is put into words. We pray because we need to hear God's response to those requests. We pray because it is only in the encounter with God that we can understand what we want and need.

Finally, real prayer is never an escape from the tasks of life. Real prayer is a necessary and invaluable preparation for the tasks of life. Without the purpose, perspective, peace of mind and compassion which come from prayer, our work won't amount to much. God defeats and destroys the work of those who labor only for themselves and for the idols of the world. Psalm 127:1 says: "Unless the Lord builds the house, those who build it labor in vain. Unless the Lord watches over the city, the watchman stays awake in vain.'' Real prayer is never an escape but rather a preparation for the work which God calls us to do in the world. Genuine prayer calls us into the world and to the tasks of the world.

But how do we deal with this deeper, more troubling, more paralyzing fear of prayer. That fear is based on our own guilt, our own lack of trust and our own reluctance to love and serve God. How do we obtain the courage, the trust, the commitment which makes prayer possible? We are in the grip of a sinful paralysis of the will which leaves us unable to save ourselves. But God can and will save us. And we have a part to play in that salvation. We can recognize and confess our inability to redeem our own souls from the power of sin. In the words of Dr. Perry LeFever, ''We are broken and we cannot by sheer willpower transform ourselves, for it is our will which must be transformed . . . . Prayer is what we do to be open to the transforming power of God.'' LeFever, Personal Viewpoint — The Theological Ground, in *LeFever, Radical Prayer* (Exploration Press, 1982) p. 86. That is why confession is so basic to our spiritual welfare. Those who confess and acknowledge their inability to help themselves, those who place their hope and their life in God's hands will be saved, redeemed and transformed. The power of God's love is so strong and so powerful that we need only let it into our lives to be changed. When we do that — when we respond to God in hope, humility and silence — all the defenses and blocks which our sinful self has so carefully and artfully erected against God's love are swept away. Then — and only then — can we pray. In the last analysis it is God who storms the last redoubt of sin and shatters the last obstacles to prayer.

Before we can pray we must be prepared to be honest and we must be prepared to submit to God's will for our life. We must be able to say: ''Thy will be done . . . . Forgive us our sins.'' That kind of honesty and commitment is only possible if we know that the God we encounter in prayer is the God of love and grace revealed in Jesus Christ. If we felt the gracious love of God in our hearts we would be able to pray. That love is all around us. God has given us our life, filled our world with color, song, beauty and human companionship. God has enabled us to sing, to think and to work. God has reached out to us in Jesus Christ, even when we were choking on our own self-centeredness and self-deception. Paul says: ''where sin increased, grace abounded all the more'' Romans 5:20. Open your eyes, open your hearts and let the grace and love of God flow into your soul. Be silent. Listen. The Holy Spirit will help you to pray. Amen.

Obstacles To Prayer?

Texts to think about: Psalm 14; Isaiah 1:10-17; 58:1-9; Matthew 6:5-6; Luke 18: 9-14; John 9:30-31

1. The sermon says that real prayer always involves self-recognition. How has prayer enabled you to understand your personal motives, desires and goals more deeply and more honestly?

2. Does prayer enable you to think about your life from a perspective beyond self?

3. Thinking about times when you have been angry, has prayer enabled you to understand the viewpoint of the person with whom you are angry?

4. Thinking about times when you are feeling successful and competent, does prayer help you understand the limitations and hazards of life? Does prayer help to keep you humble?

5. Thinking about the times when you have faced grief, has prayer comforted you? Has prayer helped you see beyond your sorrow?

6. Are there painful or unpleasant sides to your life and your personality that prayer has enabled you to understand and confront?

7. Are there positive and joyful aspects of your life that you have become conscious of through prayer?

8. How has prayer enabled you to see and become aware of God's grace working in your life?

9. Think about the effect of prayer on your emotions and feelings. The sermon suggests that prayer gives peace of mind. When has that happened in your experience? How has prayer helped you cope with such feelings as guilt, grief, ambition, anger, resentment, depression and elation?

10. Are there times when you have tried to use prayer in a "magical" way to get what you want? What have been the results?

11. The sermon says that prayer is always answered. How have your prayers been answered in ways that you hoped for? How have your prayers been answered in ways that you did not hope for?

12. How have God's answers to your prayers worked themselves out in your life in terms of your relationship with God and your relationship with those around you?

13. Does prayer make you more aware of your spiritual and emotional condition? If so, does that lead to or away from peace of mind?

14. Prayers of confession may heighten our sense of guilt. Has prayer also given you an assurance of pardon? How has your behavior and your self-image changed as a result of such prayers?

Obstacles To Prayer

George didn't want to do his homework. He wanted to go over to Pete's house and watch TV. He couldn't watch TV at his house because then he'd have to do his homework, which he did not want to do. So right after supper, George slipped out of the house and over to Pete's. He didn't ask mom or dad — as he should have — because he knew what the answer would be. It worked like a charm. No one noticed as he quietly opened the door, ran down the sidewalk and around the corner and over to Pete's house. It was great. He watched TV till 9:00 p.m. but by then he remembered that he would have to go home. Suddenly, all this didn't seem like such a good idea after all. It has been easy to slip out but how was he going to slip back in? George walked slowly back to his house and quietly opened the door. Not quietly enough, however. Mom was standing in front of him and so was dad . . .

George couldn't go out for two whole weeks and no TV! Next time George wanted to do something but he was afraid to ask because mom and dad might say no, he asked anyway because George knew it was better to be told "no" than to go ahead and do what he wanted and get punished later.

Sometimes we don't talk to God because we don't want to hear what God might say. We close our ears so we can say we didn't hear. But that doesn't work with God, any more than it worked for George when he went over to Pete's house to watch TV. It's always better to talk to God — even if we might not like what God tells us.

What Happens When We Pray?

Prayer of Meditation (read silently)

God is our refuge and strength, a very present help in trouble. Therefore we will not fear though the earth should change, though the mountains shake in the heart of the sea; though its waters roar and foam, though the mountains tremble with its tumult. The Lord of hosts is with us; the God of Jacob is our refuge (Psalm 46:1-3, 11).

Prelude

Processional

Introit

Call to Worship

Pastor:	Let us worship the God who created heavens and earth.
PEOPLE:	LET US PRAISE THE GOD WHO IS OUR MAKER AND DEFENDER!
Pastor:	Let us open our hearts and minds to the Holy One from whom no secrets are hid.
ALL:	LET US WORSHIP THE GOD WHOSE LOVE AND POWER ARE WITHOUT LIMIT.

Hymn "Behold Us Lord"

Call to Confession

Unison Prayer of Confession

Lord, we confess that we have been cold and indifferent to your love. We have not clung to you in faith and trust. We have not held your words in our heart. Too often we have sought to use prayer for our purposes and not for yours. Forgive us. Save us from our selfish indifference. Let the loving power of your word abide in us forevermore. Amen.

Assurance of Pardon

***Gloria Patri**

Announcements

Children's Sermon

***Hymn "God of Pity, God of Grace"**

Prayer of the Pastor and People

The Lord's Prayer

Anthem

Scripture Readings
Deuteronomy 9:26-29   Philippeans 1:3-6   John 15:1-7

Sermon "What Happens When We Pray?"

Silent Prayer

Offering
Offertory
*Doxology

***Hymn of Communion "O Love that Wilt Not Let Me Go"**

Benediction

***Postlude**

*indicates the congregation is to stand

What Happens When We Pray?

In the Gospel of Matthew, Jesus tells the disciples that if they have faith they can cast mountains into the sea. ". . . whatever you ask in prayer you will receive." Matthew 21:22. In John, Jesus tells the disciples: "If you abide in me, and my words abide in you, ask whatever you will, and it shall be done for you." John 15:7.

These passages are troubling for modern men and women who have some understanding of the world and the way it works. The problems were recently illustrated when Pat Robertson claimed that he turned aside a hurricane from the Florida coast by prayer. He immediately became the object of scoffing and criticism. The reaction of some of the media, and many people outside the media, was that only fools and idiots believe that prayer could change the direction of a hurricane. Our everyday experience tells us that the world does not work that way. Many of us are troubled by Robertson's claim because his description of the event implies that he personally has some special power of magic which the rest of us do not possess.[1]

Nevertheless, many of us believe, and I count myself in their number, that God does intervene in the natural world in response to prayer. So, how do we sort all this out? Can we make hurricanes, and disease, and war and famine go away by prayer? If not, are we forced to admit that prayer is simply an exercise in personal self-hypnosis — a process of auto-suggestion?

There are at least three things we need to be clear about on this subject:

First, God does act in the natural world in response to prayer.

Second, it is God who acts; not you and me. What happens is not a result of our activity but of God's activity. God may act through us if we abide in God and God's word abides in our heart, but apart from God we can do nothing.

Third, God does not act because of our very human desire to avoid suffering, pain and difficulty. God acts when and if intervention in the natural world is the way to bring human life closer to God and accomplish the reconciliation of God and God's creatures.

First, in response to prayer God does change the world around us.

A doctor friend of mine belonged to a prayer group of which I was a member. He asked one evening for our prayers in connection with a particularly difficult procedure he was to undertake the following day. We agreed that we would pray for him and his patient and we did. The next week when we gathered, he told us that he felt unusually calm and focused during the procedure. He felt that our prayers sustained him and that God was with him. What had seemed like a difficult undertaking proceeded without problem. The power of prayer had been felt in his life at that time and place and with very definite and identifiable results. Listening to my friend speak, I felt I had crossed a watershed in the journey of faith. We had prayed. God had acted. Reality had changed.

The Bible is full of accounts which testify to the action of God in the world. When John the Baptist sent his disciples to Jesus to ask if he was the Messiah, Jesus responded: "Go and tell John what you have seen and heard: the blind receive their sight, the lame walk, lepers are cleansed and the deaf hear, the dead are raised up, the poor have good news preached to them. And blessed is he that takes no offense at me." Luke 7:22-23. In that passage we hear that unexpected and miraculous events take place through and because of Jesus Christ. But those events take place as a sign, an evidence, a tangible symbol, of the power of God working in the world. They are signs which point to the Christ and to the love of God for humanity evidenced by the incarnation. The miraculous events of the New Testament are intended to point to the activity of God in Christ.

This understanding of prayer does not conflict with the world view of modern science. Modern science knows that there is real chance, real freedom and real novelty in the world. The "laws" of cause and effect are really not laws at all, but rather statements about probability which assume the exclusive power of natural forces and conditions. "Miracle" does not contradict the laws of nature because we no longer understand the natural world in terms of mechanistic laws which always and invariably apply in every case. There is indeed an order in the universe but it is not an inflexible and mechanical order.

Moreover, to the extent that natural laws explain the events of the world, they do so only in terms of the world. "Miracle" introduces a radically new element in the equation. I am impressed by the statement of Dr. Ronald Sider in an article appearing in the *Christian Century* on the Resurrection. Dr. Sider said: "Science simply tells us . . . what nature regularly does. But no amount of scientific information could, in principle, ever tell us whether there might be a God outside nature who could intervene in nature if he or she chose." *(The Christian Century,* Nov. 3, 1982, p. 1104). So there is nothing irrational about the concept of miracle. God can and does change events, conditions and persons in this world in response to prayer.

We need to understand that God acting in response to prayer can and does effect change in that portion of the world which is external to the believer. We need to know that the future really is in God's hands and is not the result of blind and mindless fate which neither knows nor cares about us.

But there are very stringent limitations which God imposes on such direct intervention in the natural world — and for very good reason. If direct divine intervention in the affairs of the world were to be anything but a highly unusual occurrence, the natural order of the universe and the consequent freedom and responsibility of human beings would be seriously undermined. The natural order of the universe is one of the greatest blessings God has given men and women. Its regular or frequent disruption would not be an act of love but rather an act of hostility towards humanity.

Second, we must be clear that in prayer it is God who acts and we who ask. By ourselves we can do nothing. Jesus says: ". . . you can not do anything apart from me." John 15:5. We have no power, no secret wisdom, no handle on the world which allows us to manipulate it as we wish. Faith is not a magic wand which we can use to obtain whatever we want. God in sovereign wisdom and love does act to alter and change the world.

We need to keep this in mind because there are understandings of prayer which are very close to blasphemy when they suggest that God is a giant vending machine into which we insert a quarter's worth of faith and from which we take away the wishes of our heart.

This distortion of prayer has been developed in its most dangerous form in Oral Roberts' doctrine of "seed faith." "Those who make a 'seed faith' gift to the Oral Roberts ministry can expect a threefold return on their 'investment' from some 'unexpected source' within a year. If they do not, Roberts promises, he will return the original contribution." Alan Brinkley, *New Republic*, Sept. 29, 1986, p. 32. If the individual contributions are small and the donor is embarrassed to admit they did not "have faith" Roberts keeps the money whether or not the promised divine largess appears. In fact, Roberts sends out multi-colored prayer sheets to be mailed back to him indicating the desires for which the donor is praying. The legend says: "The red area is for your Spiritual healing, the white area is for your physical healing, the green area is for your financial healing. Check the needs you have and rush them back to me." Brinkley, supra. Here we have the perversion of the truth that God will always give us what we want and ask for. Because God is Lord and Sovereign of the universe, our prayers are answered in accordance with God's plan for our salvation and not in accordance with our plans for worldly and financial success.

Finally, we need to understand that when God changes the objective circumstances of our life — when God heals and saves us from temporal suffering — it is not for the sake of our wealth, comfort or prosperity but for the sake of our soul. Our basic need is not to avoid pain or suffering, and certainly not to achieve ease, wealth, power or prestige. Our basic need is to be able to love God and our neighbor. It is the sickness of our soul and not the fulfillment of our financial and physical needs that is our root problem. When we encounter God in prayer we understand what it is we need and want.

When God works through prayer in our life we receive that miraculous gift which enables us to transcend our self-absorption.

When God works through prayer in our life we receive the miracle of revelation which enables us to know God's will and purpose for our life.

When God works through prayer in our life, we miraculously receive that peace of mind which enables us to endure the temptations and the hardships of life.

When God works through prayer in our life, the miracle is that we become compassionate human beings.

If a change in the external circumstances of our life will really achieve a breakthrough in the struggle against sin and evil in our life, then the miracle may happen. But it will not happen for the sake of our wallet or our physical comfort but for the sake of our soul.

It is the mountain of guilt, of selfishness, of aimlessness and loneliness which is cast into the sea in response to our prayer. Those who pray in real faith will ask for and receive what they really need: the love, the forgiveness and grace, and the redemption of Jesus Christ. That is the great and really miraculous gift which God gives to us in prayer. That is the

most important miracle that happens in prayer. The miracle
of God's grace in Jesus Christ working in our life makes all
the difference — and ultimately the only real difference — in
your life and in mine. May God grant that we abide in Christ
and that his words abide in our hearts so that the miracle of
God's forgiveness, love and grace may transform your life and
mine. Amen.

[1]In response to a question on the 700 Club on June 11, 1986, Robertson seemed to take personal
credit for changing the course of the hurricane. ". . . If I couldn't move a hurricane, I could
hardly move a nation."

What Happens When We Pray?

Texts to think about: Exodus 14:5-30; Isaiah 36:1—37:38; Matthew 7:7-13, 21:22; Luke 11:15-18; James 5:16

1. **The sermon says that because of prayer the "objective situation" — the problem "out there" — disease, attitudes of others, threats to our income — sometimes changes. Has this ever happened in your life? Do you feel that you have been healed by prayer? What effect has this "deliverance" had on your relationship with God and with those around you?**

2. **When you pray that the problem "out there" will go away and it doesn't, how do you react? Do you believe that if you had had more faith, the result would have been different? Do you believe that God "punishes" lack of faith by refusing to answer prayer?**

3. **The sermon also says God can change our attitude of understanding of the "objective situation" — the problem "out there" — so that we experience and deal with it differently than we would otherwise have done. Has this changed in your life? Describe how prayer changed your experience of the problem. What were the long term results of that experience?**

4. **Are there times when simply telling God about your problem helps you to face and deal with the problem?**

5. Are there dangers to your spiritual life in believing that God can change the objective situation through prayer? What are those dangers and how can you avoid them?

6. Think back to a time when someone prayed for you. How was your relationship with that person changed?

7. When you pray for others, does your attitude and behavior toward that person change? If so, how?

8. If you have ever had the experience of having prayers of intercession answered, how has this changed your relationship with the person for whom you prayed?

9. In thinking about why you don't pray, would you say it is because you are afraid your prayers won't be answered or because you are afraid they might be answered?

10. The sermon speaks of an "encounter with God." Do you feel that you have had such an encounter? Are there words which could help others understand what that experience was like for you?

11. How would you describe whatever reality you have encountered in prayer?

12. The sermon says that real prayer is always answered. Have you found this to be true in your own experience? How have your prayers been answered? What have you learned about yourself, about God and about the world from the answers you have received?

13. Are there specific and tangible prayer requests which have been fulfilled? What are they?

14. Do you think things actually turned out differently because of your prayer?

15. The sermon suggests that prayer raises our petitions to the level of consciousness and thus enables both God and ourselves to deal with these petitions in a more creative and honest way. Have you found this to be the case? How has that worked in your life?

What Happens When We Pray?

George had to give a speech on "Indians of the Northwest" in school. He had read the books in the library that Mrs. Schmidt, his teacher, had helped him find. He had made an outline of the talk he was going to give. He had done everything he was supposed to do to prepare. The problem was he was scared to death. He didn't want to admit he was scared. In fact, he told Pete he wasn't scared at all! But that wasn't true. He was so scared he felt sick to his stomach when he thought about it. Mom noticed it. Dad noticed it. The closer the day came, the worse George felt. The night before the day when George was supposed to give his speech, mom and dad and George said a prayer. It was short and simple. "Please God, help George not to be afraid. Stand beside him and help him tomorrow."

The next day when George got up something was different. He didn't feel nearly so scared. Maybe a little nervous, but not scared. And when he got up in front of the class he looked right at Pete, who was sitting in the back row and making faces at him, and began to talk. As soon as he heard the sound of his own voice he knew he would be okay. And he was. In a few minutes the report was over and George sat down. He had done well. But George learned a lot more from giving that report than the facts about Indians. He learned that in God he had a friend who could and would help him. It was a lesson George never forgot and I hope you won't either.

Order Of Service
What Should We Pray For?

Prayer of Meditation (read silently)

   . . . the steadfast love of the Lord is from everlasting to everlasting upon those who fear him, and his righteousness to children's children, to those who keep his commandments (Psalm 103:17-18).

Call to Worship

> Pastor: Let us turn in faith and gratitude to the God who loves and cares for us.
>
> PEOPLE: LET US PRAY TO THE LORD FOR DIRECTION AND GUIDANCE!
>
> Pastor: Let us worship the Holy One of Israel who leads us in the ways of righteousness and delivers us from the power of evil.
>
> ALL: LET US WORSHIP GOD FOR THE LORD IS OUR HOPE AND OUR SALVATION. IN GOD'S WORD WE TRUST FOR THE SOVEREIGN'S POWER ENDURES FOREVER. GOD'S GRACE AND MERCY ARE SUFFICIENT FOR ALL OUR NEEDS.

Hymn "Open Now Thy Gates of Beauty"

Call to Confession

Unison Prayer of Confession

   Gracious God, hear our prayer! We often do not know what to ask for. Our petitions are often confused, uncertain and half-hearted. We ask without ourselves being willing to work for that which we seek. We are not able to make your will our own. Forgive us and teach us to pray with our whole heart and mind. We ask in Jesus' name. Amen.

Assurance of Pardon

***Gloria Patri**

Announcements

Children's Sermon

***Hymn** "What a Friend We Have in Jesus"

Prayer of the Pastor and People

The Lord's Prayer

Anthem

Scripture Readings
    Isaiah 2:1-4   John 17:15-19   James 5:13-15

Sermon "What Shall We Pray For?"

Silent Prayer

Offering
    Offertory
    *Doxology

***Hymn** "In Christ There is No East or West"

Benediction

Choral Response (congregation seated)

***Postlude**

*indicates the congregation is to stand

What Should We Pray For?

Several years ago a religious magazine carried the story of an accused arsonist who had been arrested by the Canadian police for setting a fire. Alone in his cell, the forlorn and desperate man fell to his knees and uttered what is probably-one of the oldest and most sincere of all prayers: "Lord, let me get away with it just this once!" Unfortunately for him, the cell was bugged. At the trial the local prosecutor sought to admit the prayer in evidence as a confession. The trial judge overruled the objection and the prayer came into evidence. So perhaps my first caution should be that prayers for the avoidance of conviction of crime should be prayed in private.

In a more serious and, I hope, relevant vein, we do need to ask what we should pray for. We should ask first for those things which are in our heart and mind. We should ask that we be forgiven and that we be able to forgive others. We should pray that we be delivered from the power of temptation. Because prayer brings us close to all those in want and close to God, we pray that God's kingdom come and that God's will be done on earth as in heaven.

We should pray for that which is on our hearts. We should pray for the genuine concerns of our life. When we are fearful and anxious, we should pray for peace and courage. When we are injured or ill we should pray for healing and health. When we are sad and depressed because of our loved ones, we should pray for them and their welfare. When we face some great decision which taxes our wisdom and our understanding, our judgment and our insight, we should pray for guidance.

Such prayers are both inevitable and desirable. They are inevitable because we can not avoid concern about our lives and the welfare of those who are close to us. God loves us and gladly shares the burden of those concerns with us in prayer. We turn to God in these situations as naturally and as confidently as a child turns to its parent in times of trouble and danger. We need never fear that God is too remote, or too good, or too busy, or too concerned with cosmic issues to hear our prayer and our concern.

At the end of his reign, David was betrayed by his beloved son Absolom and by his chief advisor. In that dark hour David prayed that the advice received by his foes might be turned to foolishness. Solomon, faced with the responsibility for a kingdom far beyond his experience or maturity, prayed for wisdom. General Patton, racing to the relief of the beleaguered American garrison in Bastogne in World War II, prayed for the weather to clear so that the surrounded American forces could be supplied by air. These prayers show us that we should put aside all reserve, all hesitation and all doubt. Such prayer may well be the first stage — the first step — in our prayer life. But it is an important and natural first step. We should boldly take that step in confidence and trust. Pray fervently, constantly and with determination for the concerns and needs which are close to your heart.

But beyond the immediate concerns of our daily life we pray that we be forgiven and that we are able to forgive others. We pray that the broken strands of our relationship with God and with others be mended and renewed. We pray that we be delivered from the burden of animosity, resentment and hostility which works like an addictive poison to misshape and deform our life. One of the saddest things a minister can hear is the account of some long passed slight or hurt told in a way which makes it plain that the event may be half a century old in chronological time but is only minutes old in psychological time. The face tenses, the jaw tightens, the voice trembles. Suddenly the pastor knows that the problem is not the hurt but the inability to let go of the hurt and let the past be the past.

We pray that we be forgiven our sins. We pray that all those wrongs, done intentionally or unintentionally, wrongs done because of our inability to see, to love, to care, be forgiven. We pray that, in the words of Psalm 103, "our sins be cast far from us."

The only thing that is as sad as the damage done by our inability to forgive is the anguish we suffer because we feel we are not forgiven for past wrongs we have done. The burden of guilt which is carried through life is enormous and terrible in its consequences. It prevents us from renewing our relationships with those we love. It cripples our ability to live and love. We know that the hurt we have done others is also an injury to God because it is an injury to one whom God loves. Therefore, we need to pray that we can be forgiven by those we love. We also need to pray that God restore us to his favor and that, for the sake of Jesus Christ, the grace of God may cover our iniquities.

But beyond the repair and restoration of our relationship to God and to those around us, we pray that we be delivered from the power of evil. "Lead us not into temptation" is a prayer that God will shatter the illusions, unmask the lies and expose the deceit which is always at the heart of evil. Evil can only thrive in our life if it is protected by self-deception and denial. To be delivered from temptation is to be enabled to see our life in terms of its relationship to God and neighbor. It is to know that the fulfillment of our life, our true peace and happiness, lies in that solidarity, that justice, that truth and honesty, that compassion which the Bible means by righteousness. To be delivered from temptation is to be able to see the harm which our greed, our lust, our ambition and pride inflict on others and to feel that harm as harm to ourselves. To be delivered from temptation is to be enabled to see that harm to others is ultimately harm to ourselves.

Still, we need to take one further step if our prayer life is to be complete.

The God to whom we turn with child-like confidence and trust is the God who redeems, transforms and redirects our life. In prayer God leads, directs and supports us. In prayer God changes the direction and the purpose of our life. The encounter with God is always a transforming and renewing encounter — a life giving encounter. Because of that renewal, that redirection, that redemption and transformation, the goals and objects which we seek — the petitions which we offer to and through God — also change.

Because prayer changes our perspective and our understanding, we come to realize that in the truest and deepest sense our spiritual and material welfare — the fulfillment and completion of our life — is dependent on the welfare of others and their ability to fulfill their lives. In prayer we come to love God and our neighbor. When we love others and love God we know that our welfare and their welfare can never be separated.

In the end our prayer is that God's kingdom come.

We pray for that peace and justice in the world which will be the end of violence, cruelty and hatred and bring in the reign of justice, mercy and freedom for all peoples.

We pray that the evil and ominous growth of all weapons of destruction — thermonuclear, chemical and biological — will not destroy our planet. We pray that our lakes and streams, our forests and cities, our music, our churches and our human bodies will not become a cosmic funeral pyre and our planet left floating like a huge charred casket through the darkness of space.

We pray that the blind, mindless, stupidity of terrorism and the conditions which give rise to that terrorism, will pass away.

We pray that the grinding, hopeless, paralyzing poverty which spreads like a deadly pestilence across so much of the world will give way to the prosperity and plenty which God intends for all men and women. We pray that in place of distended stomachs and the vacant stare of eyes dulled by starvation, the children of the world may know the nutrition of milk, the satisfaction of bread, and the warmth of a woolen blanket to protect their bodies against the cold.

We pray that the nightmare of secret police, death squads and repressive political systems of Right and Left, in Central America, China, Africa and the Near East, give way to order, liberty and freedom. We pray that men and women be able to speak and write freely and that they be able to worship in accordance with their conscience.

We pray that the odious and hateful system of apartheid and all discrimination based on race, on color and on creed shall vanish and that all men and women be accorded with dignity, the respect and the liberty which is their God-given right. We pray that peace and justice become a reality for all men and women.

We pray that we may be made whole and complete. We pray that God's love fill our hearts and that we find that peace and tranquility which comes only when we are reconciled to God. We pray that at last our heart may rest in the loving heart of God and that we find that peace which passes all understanding. Amen.

What Should We Pray For?

Texts to think about: Psalm 6; Psalm 137:7-9; 2 Samuel 15:31, 17:1-14; Matthew 6:5-15; John 17:1-26, Acts 7:54-60

1. Thinking back on the last few years of your life, list some of the things that you have prayed for.

2. What kinds of things do you ask for yourself in prayer?

3. Do you spend time regularly praying for others?

4. Do you tell the person for whom you are praying that you are doing so?

5. How have your prayer requests for yourself and others changed over the past few years?

6. Is there a correlation between the frequency of your prayer and the kinds of things you ask for?

7. Has prayer enabled you to forgive others?

8. Has prayer enabled you to feel and accept the forgiveness of others?

9. How have the changes in your own self-understanding resulting from prayer contributed to your reconciliation with others?

10. How have the changes in your self-understanding contributed to your ability to accept God's forgiveness and the forgiveness of others?

11. Have you been able to pray for those who persecute you? "Persecution" sounds extreme — but can you pray for people who you know are intent on doing harm, physical or emotional, to you? If you have been able to pray for your enemies, how have such prayers changed your attitude toward such persons? How have such prayers helped to heal the wounds and the hurts which they have caused you?

12. How has prayer enabled you to confront and defeat temptation? Has prayer removed the temptation or has it allowed you to withstand the temptation without yielding?

13. What are some of the larger social and "political" problems which you address in prayer?

14. What part do you believe prayer plays in constructive social change?

15. Does praying for the kingdom bring the kingdom closer? How might that happen?

What Should We Pray For?

George was playing ball in the lot with Pete over behind the school when it happened. He heard the screech of car tires and heard a half bark, half howl that sounded like Dash. Without even bothering to pick up his bat, George cut across the school yard, down the street and around the corner. There was Dash lying by the side of the road. Mom was already there. Dash looked terrible. He was in a lot of pain. "Stay here," mom said. "I'm going to call Dr. Sanders, the veterinarian." George and Pete looked at Dash. "Please God, let Dash be okay" George heard himself say. Just then mom came back. Pete, George and mom carefully lifted Dash on a blanket and carried him into the office. "Mom," George asked, "Does God care about Dash?" "God cares about Dash and God cares about you" mom answered. "God has heard your prayer and God will do what's best."

Dash did get better. George always remembered what happened. It made him feel a lot better knowing that you could pray to God — even for your dog — without being in a church. It was good to know that you could ask for what was really most important to you. And it made George feel even better knowing that God heard and cared and that God would do what was best.

Order Of Service
Seven Suggestions For A Better Prayer Life

Silent Prayer

O Lord, hear me praying; listen to my plea, O God my King, for I will never pray to anyone but you. I know you get no pleasure from wickedness and cannot tolerate the slightest sin. But make everyone rejoice who puts his trust in you. Keep them shouting for joy because you are defending them. Fill all who love you with your happiness. For you bless the godly man, O Lord; you protect him with your shield of love (Psalm 5:1-4, 11-12).

Prelude

Responsive Call to Worship†

Pastor: The grace of our Lord Jesus Christ and the love of God and the communion of the Holy Spirit be with you all.

PEOPLE: AND ALSO WITH YOU.

Hymn ''Holy, Holy, Holy''

Call to Confession

Unison Prayer of Confession

We have promised to live as your people, God. Yet we confess that we fail you and one another. We do not honor one another as we should. We refuse your cry for help in the voices of the poor and hungry. We have not been faithful to the trust you have placed in us. Merciful God, receive us as we are and forgive us. Encourage us with your love that we may commit ourselves anew to live as those who belong to you; through the grace of Jesus Christ. Amen.

Assurance of Pardon

Announcements

Children's Sermon

***Hymn** "Come Thou Almighty King"

Prayer of the Pastor and People

The Lord's Prayer

Special Music

Scripture Readings
    2 Kings 5:1-15a   Colossians 2:6-15   Luke 11:1-3

Sermon "Seven Suggestions For A Better Prayer Life"

Offering
    Offertory
    *Doxology

***Hymn** "Come, We Who Love the Lord"

Benediction

***Postlude**

*indicates the congregation is to stand

†From *Book of Worship*, United Church of Christ (1986) p. 277.

Seven Suggestions For A Better Prayer Life

Of all the spiritual disciplines, prayer is probably the most important and yet one of the least understood. For many people it has become an empty convention. For others, it is a very uncomfortable experience because we have the feeling that something is supposed to be happening and isn't. Many people feel like prayer is a one-way phone conversation in which they are talking into a line with no one on the other end. It's not so much that our prayers aren't answered as the feeling, which we are often too embarrassed to admit, that they probably haven't been heard at all.

So the petition of the disciples is still one which comes to ministers, priests and rabbis — teach me to pray.

Some time ago I preached an entire series of sermons on prayer — why we pray, what happens when we pray, what we should pray for — and I am still willing to stick by what I said then. But I don't intend to repeat that sermon series. Nor do I intend to presume to "teach" you how to pray. Only God can really do that. Instead, I want to undertake a more modest but still important task. I want to offer some specific suggestions for prayer — suggestions that may help your prayer life become more vital and faith-sustaining.

First, if you notice the prayer which Jesus taught the disciples, you will find that it is brief. In this respect it differs from the traditional ceremonial prayers used in the synagogue of the day. Many words are not necessary in prayer. Nor is literary or rhetorical skill of any particular advantage. What is important is that the words come from our heart, that they express our deepest feelings, fears, desires and hopes. A few words spoken with sincerity and from the heart are far better than many words — no matter how beautiful they may be — which really amount only to so much idle chatter.

Second, don't try to hide your feelings from God. Honesty is the basis for all communication. When you try and hide your feelings from God you are also hiding them from yourself. If you are angry, let your anger be expressed in your prayer — even if your anger is directed at God. God can handle anger — thank goodness. But it is difficult for us to hear or understand God's response to our prayer unless we have spoken honestly to God. If you are frightened, let your fear be expressed. If you are jealous and envious, let that jealousy and envy be evident. Only as you hear yourself give expression to your feelings will you begin to understand those feelings yourself. And it is only as you begin to understand your own feelings will you be able to hear what God wants to say to you about those feelings.

Third, allow time for silent reflections on what you have said. Wait for God's answer. Do not be afraid of silence. Do not feel that you are required to fill up the voids of silence with chatter, explanation or rationalization. Make room for silence in your prayer so that you can begin to listen to what God has to say and so you can really hear yourself say what it is you have said. It is important to listen to yourself just as it is important to listen to God. Listening is as important in prayer as speaking. Listen to yourself. Listen for God speaking to you. Remember that prayer is dialogue, not monologue.

Fourth, be alert to how God answers prayer. Understand that the answers to prayer usually come in and through that "still, small voice" which speaks with incredible power and which is evident in a tremendous conviction about what we are to do or refrain from doing in the particular situation. However, God does not always tell us what to do. God may decline to direct us for the simple reason that God may choose to let us struggle with and take responsibility for our decision ourself. That does not mean that our prayer has not been answered. It means that God wants you to make the decision and to take responsibility for that decision. That does not mean that our prayer has not been heard; it merely indicates that our request has been declined. Faith is what enables us to believe that even such an answer is indeed the right answer for us in that situation. The appropriate prayer then is that God use your decision for the best. Remember: we are called to be faithful; not infallible. God can use our mistakes just as well as our "correct" decisions provided they represent our best effort made in faith and trust.

Do not expect an audible reply. That can and sometimes does happen, but it is unusual. The answers that come in and through prayer come as a result of listening to what we have said and in reflecting on what we have said. God often speaks through our reflections and our insights into our own petitions and requests.

Fifth, pray regularly. Do not wait for some disaster or crisis to devastate your life before you turn to prayer. It may be true that there are no atheists in foxholes but it's hard to pray for anything except your own short term survival when you are hip deep in mud and shells are exploding overhead. Prayer which grows out of a severe and immediate crisis is sincere but it is very limited in scope. There is something terribly defective about a relationship in which the only communication takes place when one party desperately needs the help of the other. Moreover, prayer in such circumstances seems unfamiliar and strange. Set aside a regular time to pray. It need not be a long period. Pray. Meditate on your prayer and pray again. Fifteen minutes may be enough. If you are unable to pray, sit and meditate in silence on that inability. But make prayer a regular, normal and important part of your life.

Sixth, begin prayer with thanksgiving. Pause to consider what God has already done for you. Gratitude and humility, Reinhold Niebuhr said, are the two foundations of faith. It's easy to pray in the hospital before the surgery; it is not nearly so often that we remember to give thanks in prayer after things have worked out and our initial prayers of petition have been answered in the way we hoped they would be. One of the reasons we sometimes feel our prayers aren't answered is because we so seldom pause to consider what God has already done for us.

Seventh, pray with others. Joining with others in prayer will enrich your own prayer life. God works through those who pray together. Solitary prayer is good; prayer with others is even better. By praying with others we come to understand them and to know them in a very intimate way. We come to see what God is doing in their life as well as our own. This kind of spiritual sharing gives perspective to our prayer life and prevents us from misguided and overly subjective misunderstandings. A stable and healthy prayer life requires a horizontal as well as a vertical dimension.

There are no magic techniques for making prayer "work." Prayer is essentially dialogue with God and with ourselves. Like all dialogue, to be fruitful it must be undertaken in a deliberate and serious way. The disciplines of prayer are simply those means by which we open ourselves to participation in that dialogue with God — with that mysterious and powerful Other who is both within us and beyond us.

If salvation is really a relationship of intimacy with and devotion to God, then prayer is both a means to and an evidence of salvation. It is my prayer that we will all learn to be more disciplined, more intentional and more serious about our dialogue with God. Amen.

Seven Suggestions For A Better Prayer Life

Texts to think about: Psalm 5; Luke 11:1-4, 16:19-31, 18:9-14; Romans 8:26, 12:12, 15:30-33

1. The sermon says that it is not the eloquence but the sincerity of our words which are important in prayer. Are words necessary at all? Are they helpful? Why?

2. Do you pray when you are angry? Have you ever prayed for something bad to happen to another person? What happened to them? What happened to you?

3. In your prayer life, how much time do you spend listening to yourself and to God? Do you always initiate the dialogue with God? Do you ever simply present yourself to God and wait for God to initiate the dialogue with you?

4. How have you experienced the answers which God gives you in prayer? How do those answers come to you?

5. How regular are you in prayer? Do you pray only in "tight" situations when you need help badly? Do you regard daily prayer as a burden and a chore? What would have to happen to change your attitude about regular prayer? Do you set aside a particular time to pray each day? Do you pray briefly and silently during the day?

6. How much time do you spend in prayer asking for things
   and how much time do you spend giving thanks for things
   God has already done for you? Are you able to give thanks
   when your petitions are not answered as you would wish?

7. Do you regularly pray with others? How do you keep these
   times from becoming "therapy sessions?" How has prayer
   with others affected your relationship with them? Should
   such prayer groups be limited in time? Do they tend to become "exclusive"? If they do, is that good or bad? How
   might this be avoided?

Seven Suggestions For A Better Prayer Life

George's school counselor was someone you could talk to if you had a problem. His name was Mr. Prescott. George had never talked to him. He knew he was there. He had walked by Mr. Prescott's office almost every day at school. But he never had talked to him. Now George was standing outside the door of Mr. Prescott's office feeling very nervous. He needed to get special permission to park his bike inside the building. George was staying with his grandma and grandpa for a week while his mom and dad were away. Grandma and grandpa lived about three miles from school and that meant that he would have to ride his bike. The problem was that the bike was a really nice ten speed and George was afraid something might happen to it if he left it outside in the bike rack. But if he could put it inside the boiler room and lock it, everything would be okay.

George had to get permission from Mr. Prescott to do that. How would he explain all that to Mr. Prescott? What if Mr. Prescott said "no." George was still standing in front of the office when the door opened and there was Mr. Prescott! "Hi, George," he said "Can I help you?" "Uhhh, Uhhh, yeah, I guess so . . ." George mumbled. Mr. Prescott looked and sounded so friendly that George managed to tell him about his problem. "I think we can arrange for that" Mr. Prescott said. George breathed a sigh of relief. Talking to Mr. Prescott wasn't so tough after all, he thought.

Maybe God is a little bit like Mr. Prescott. We have trouble talking to God because we pass by the door but never bother to go in and meet him. Then, when we have a real need to talk to God, it seems strange and difficult. Maybe if we prayed more often, we might find that God was even more kindly and more willing to help than George found Mr. Prescott to be.